Aurora & Grace
By Avant Garde Theatre of Dance

213 W Ennis Ave. Ennis, TX 75119
(469) 749-7969

Written & Edited by
Sarah Austin
Christopher Brown

© Copyright 2020 Avant Garde Theatre of Dance, LLC. All Rights Reserved. This was designed and published by Avant Garde Theatre of Dance in Ennis, Texas. For more information please visit avantgardetheatre.com.

This Book Belongs To:

———————————— ✦ ————————————

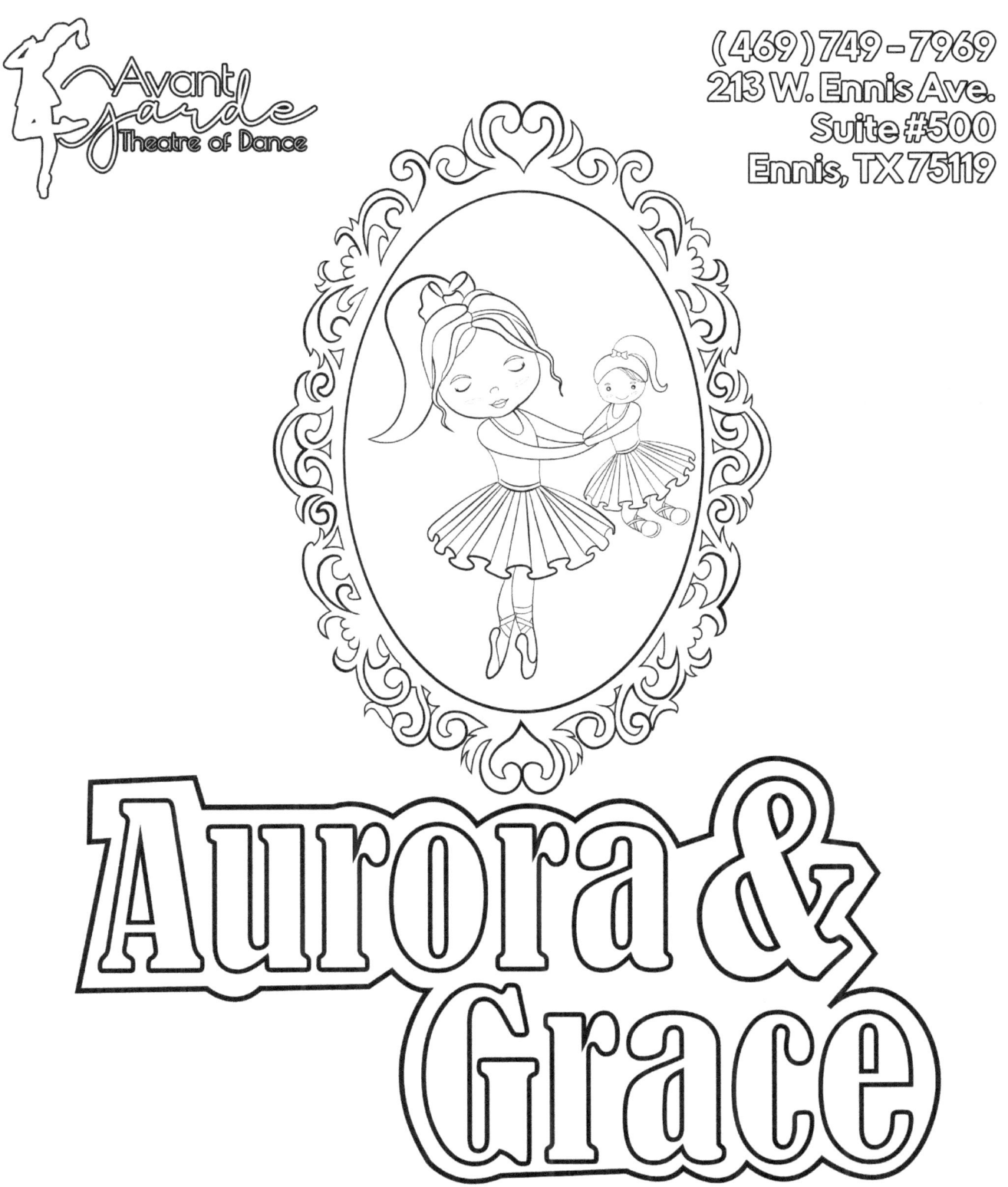

Aurora & Grace

By Avant Garde Theatre of Dance

avantgardetheatreofdance.com

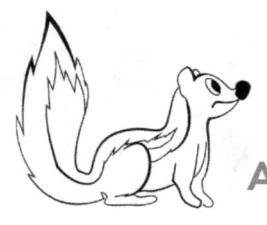

Aurora is six years old and lives in Ennis, Texas.

She wants to be a ballerina, to dance and wear pretty dresses.

Her mommy, daddy, Grammy and Grampy love to see her shows.

Even Mr. Rabbit and Mr. Squirrel come to watch her plie like a pro.

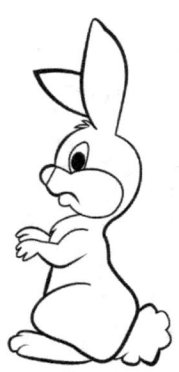

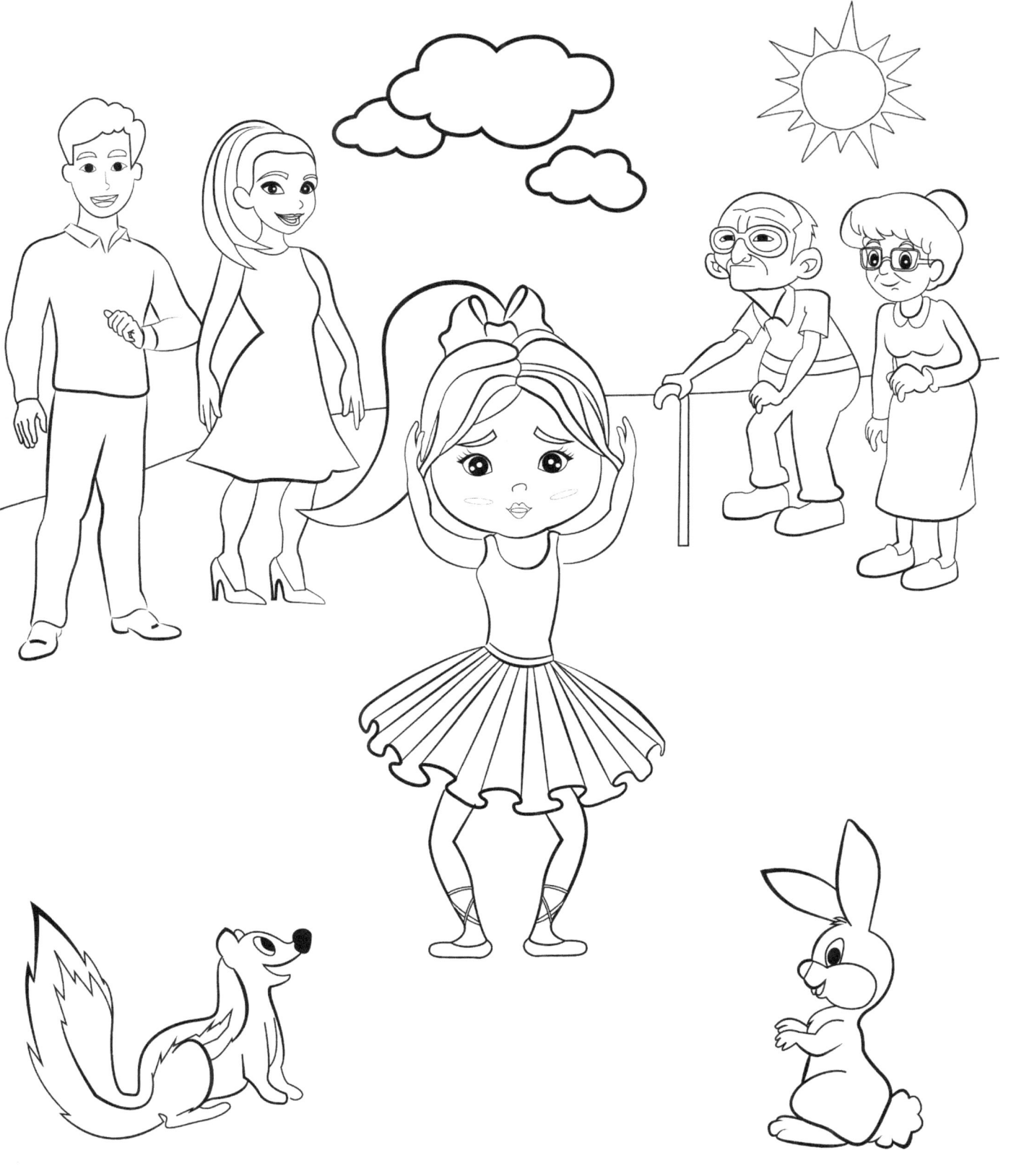

Not every performance goes as planned.

Aurora bent too far and her knees hit the sand.

Grammy ran over like she was in a race.

she gave Aurora a magic doll and said, "her name is Grace,

"she will help you to dance and learn to be strong."

Aurora smiled and wrapped her tight in her arms.

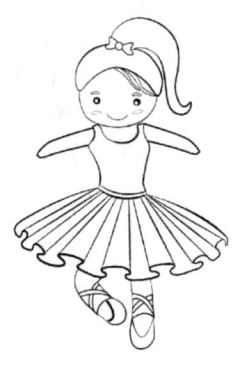

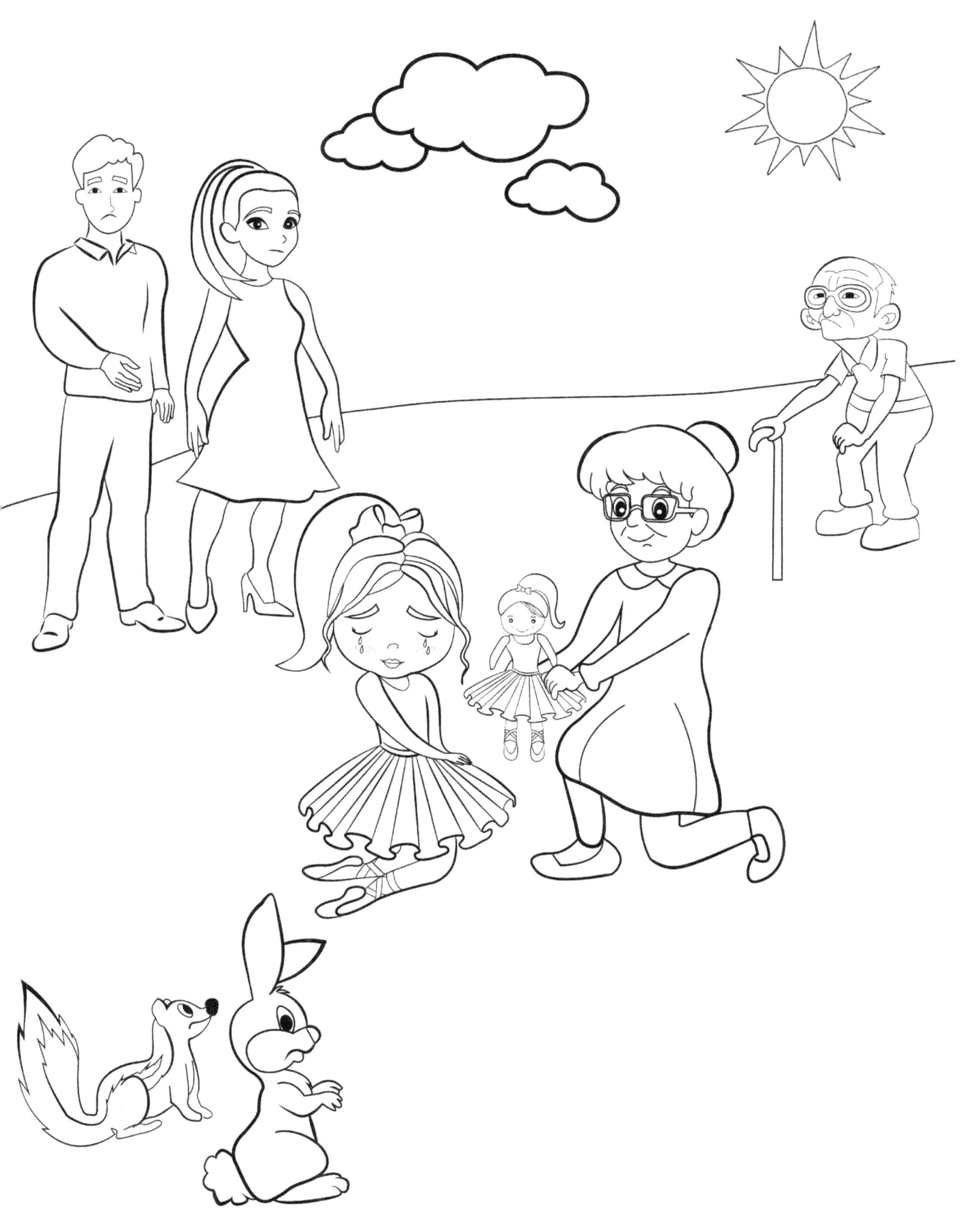

Aurora jumped, danced, and turned holding onto Grace's hands.

It wasn't too long before they were best friends.

All day long Aurora danced in her room.

Until mommy came in and said "its time for bed, you have to get up soon."

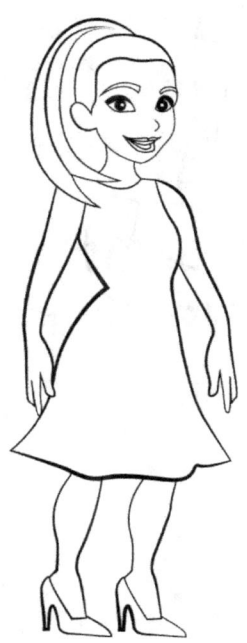
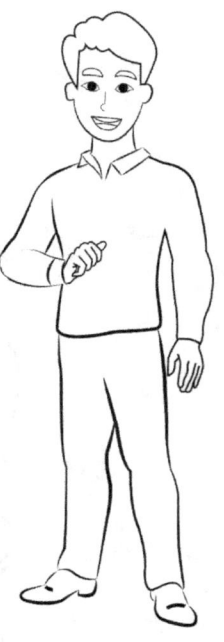

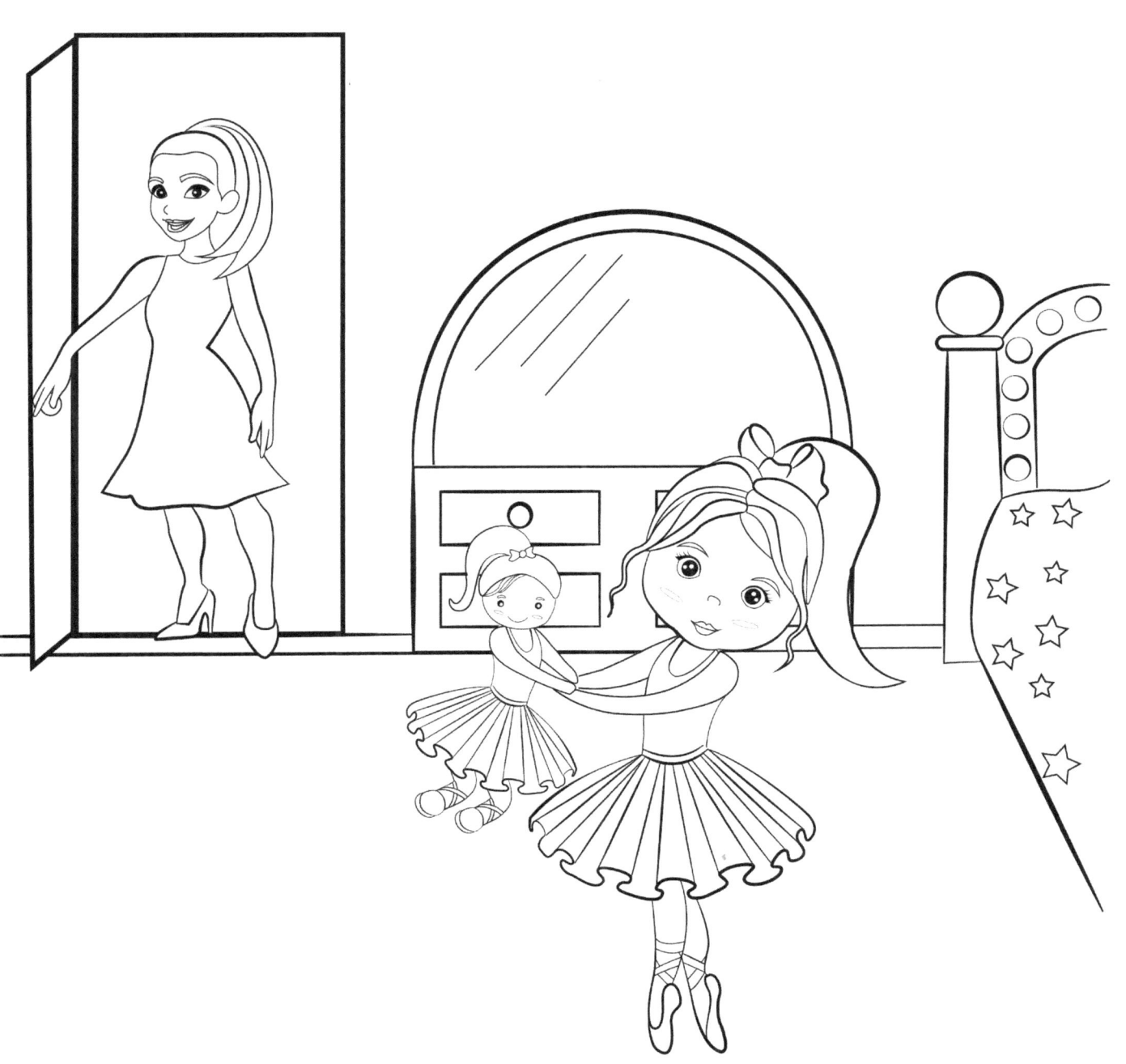

Aurora laid her head down and closed her eyes.

And a few moments later there was a huge surprise!

Grace came alive and started to dance.

The magic was real and this was Aurora's chance.

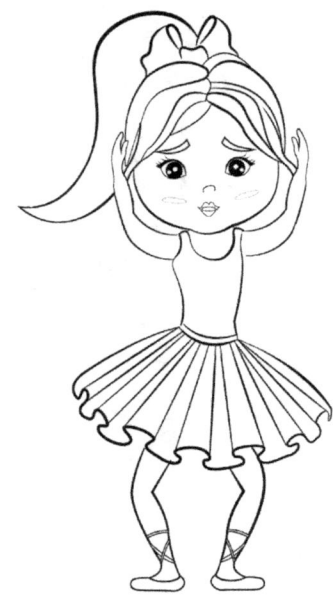

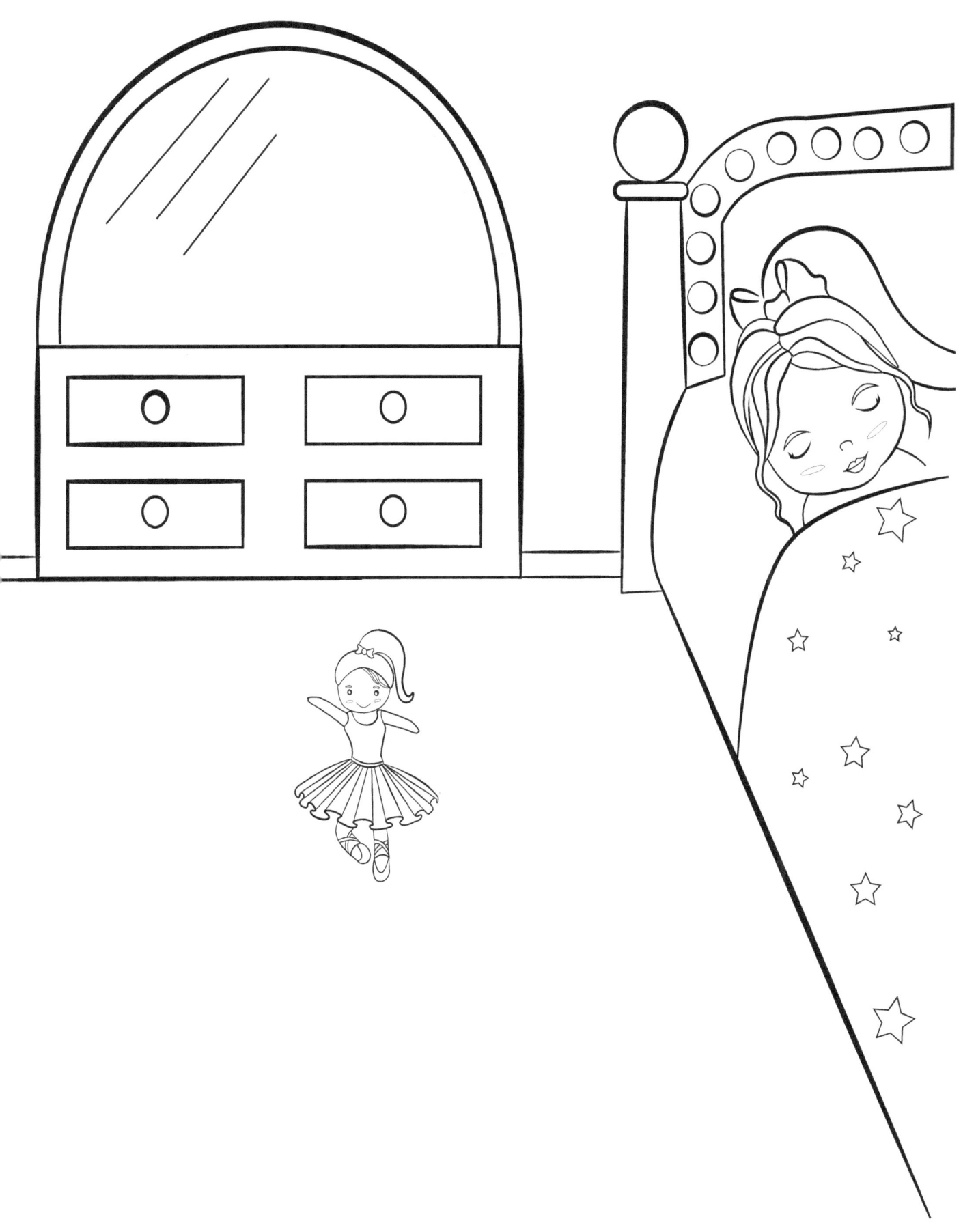

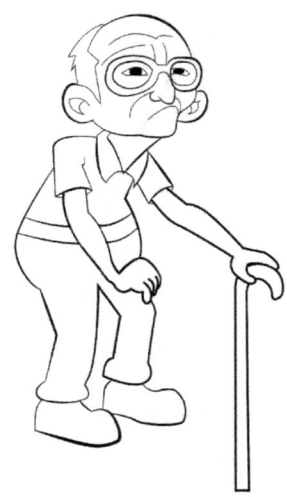

Grace showed her steps, like passe and arabesque.

With a little practice and some magic, she was sure to be the best.

They practiced and danced until the rise of the sun.

They decided to do a grand finale, that would be so much fun!

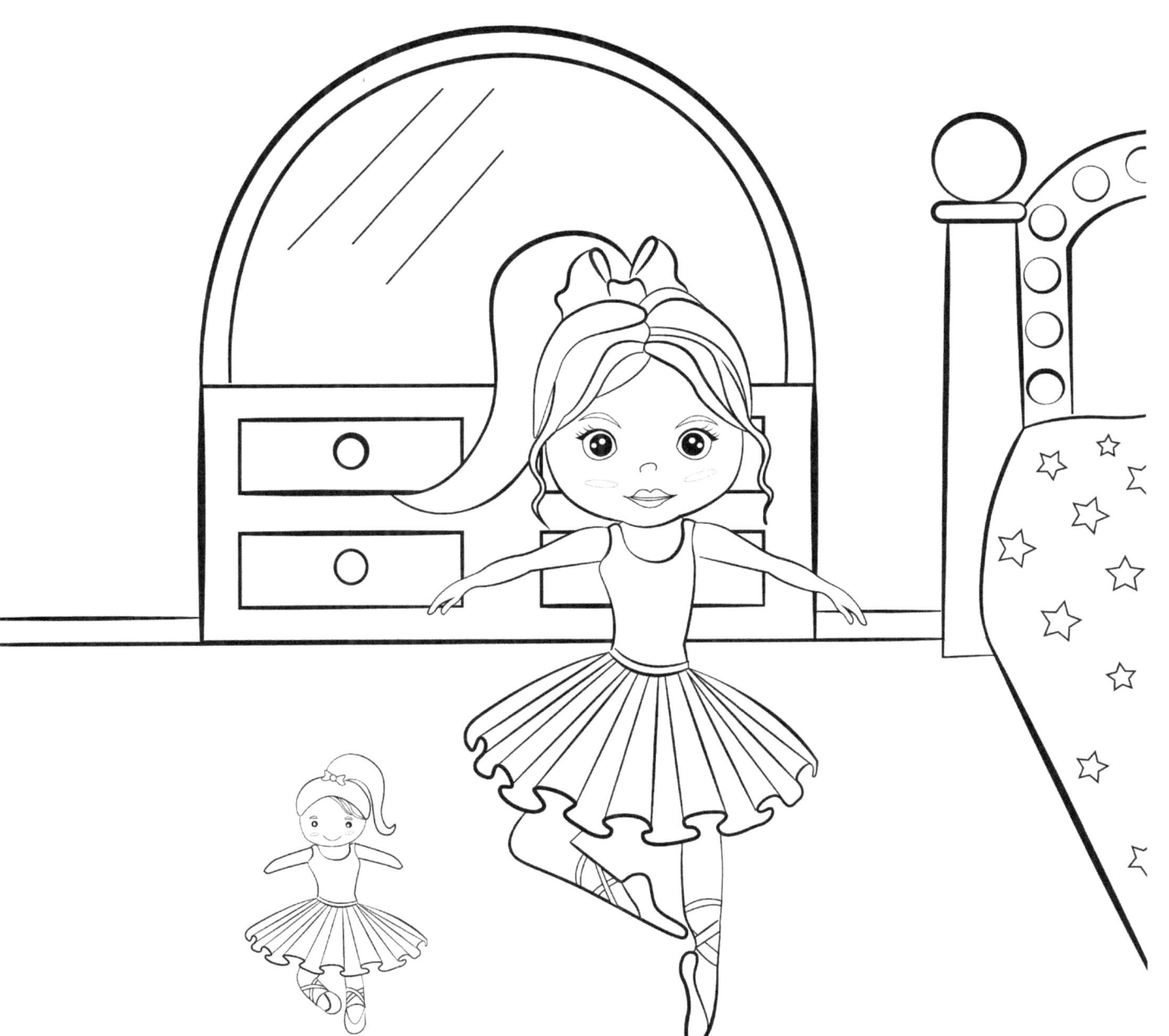

They did a huge show and everyone came.

Grampy got so excited he dropped his cane.

Mr. Rabbit and Mr. Squirrel cheered and cheered.

Mommy and daddy were so proud they shed a tear.

Grammy just smiled and whispered "I told you..."

And as they bowed Aurora hugged Grace and said "I love you!"

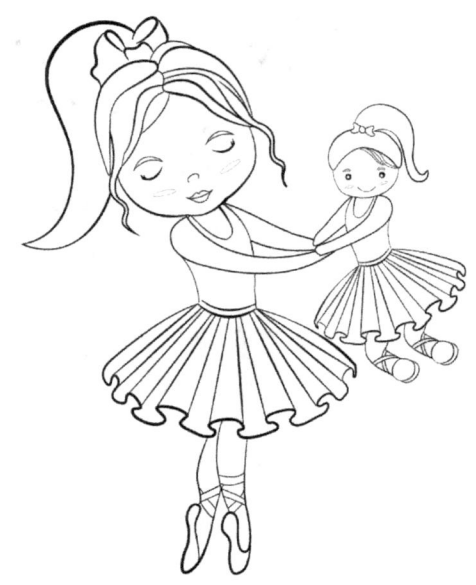

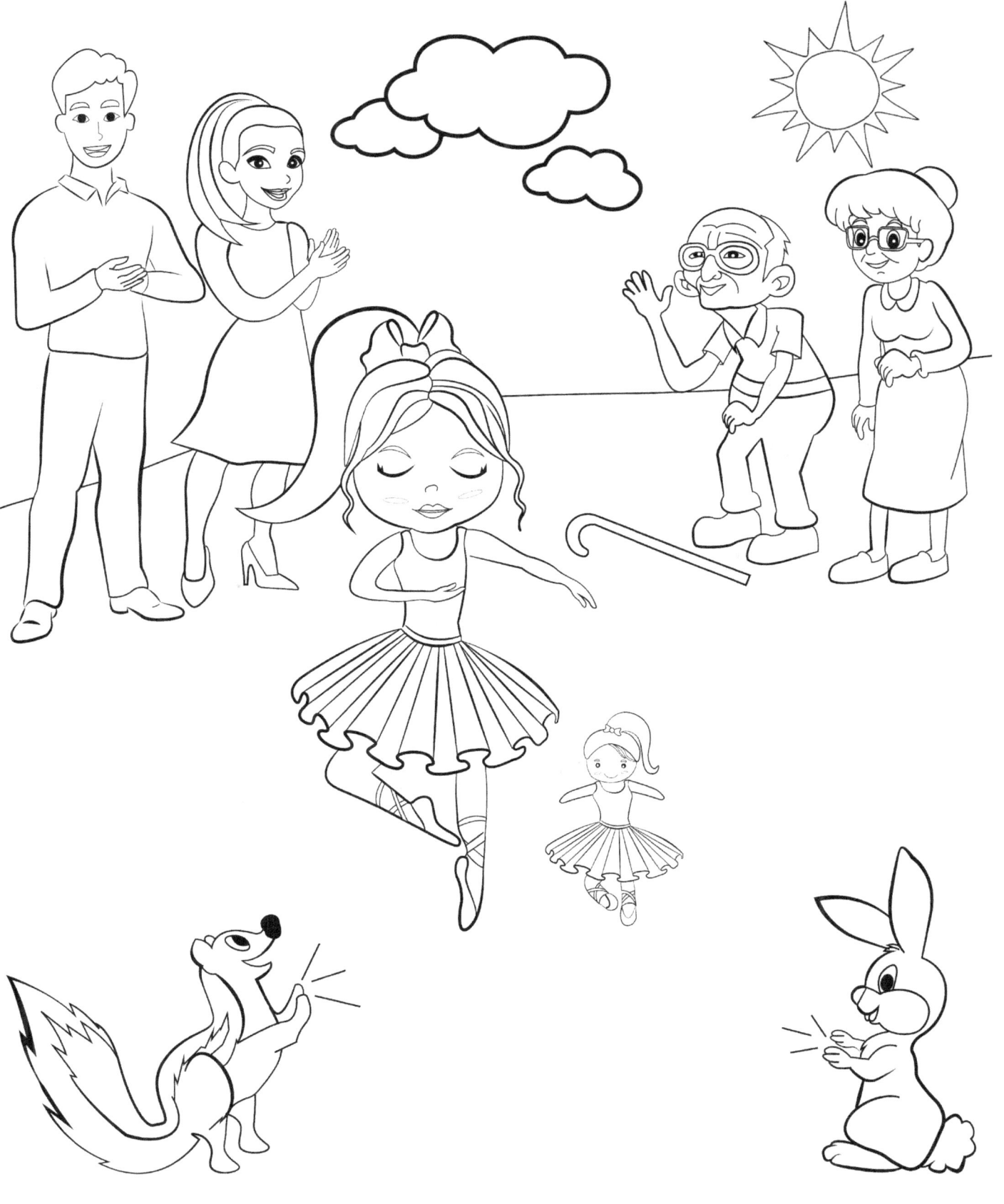

THE END

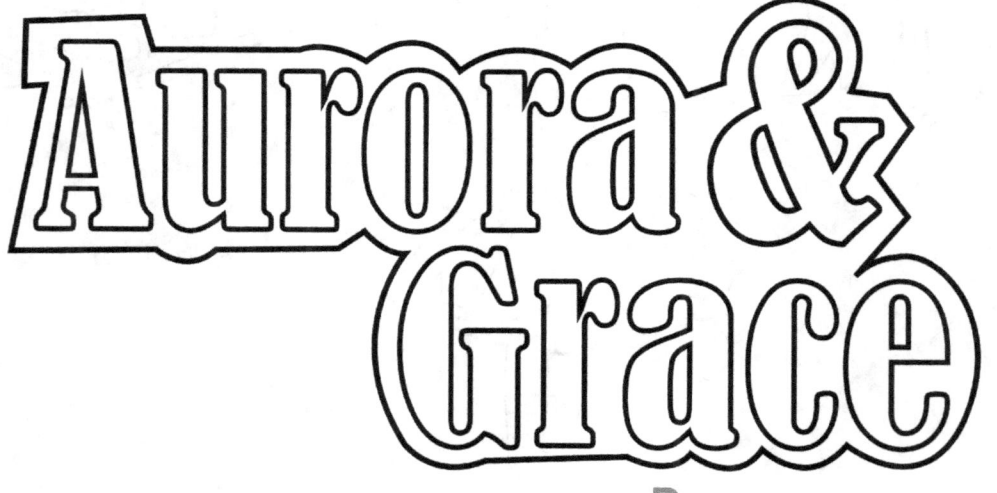

By
Avant Garde Theatre of Dance

Can you draw Aurora hugging Grace after the Grand Finale?

Help Mr. Rabbit and Mr. Squirrel find all of the Ballet Terms!

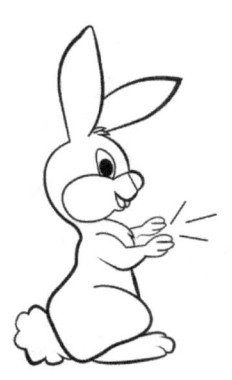

```
E C B N P G O H O K
G P A S U R W I M I
R A A S B A L L E T
A L C S S C B H F G
A A T K S E L S C D
U T U F R E M M A P
R E T K W Q N B U L
O N U A J U F E L I
R D P O I N T E L E
A U B A R R E F P M
```

Assemble   Pointe   Ballet   Barre
Passe   Aurora   Tendu   Grace
Plie   Tutu

avantgardetheatreofdance.com

Create your own Aurora!

Choose a color for each number below. Then, color Aurora using the colors you chose for each number!

1 _____   2 _____   3 _____

4 _____   5 _____

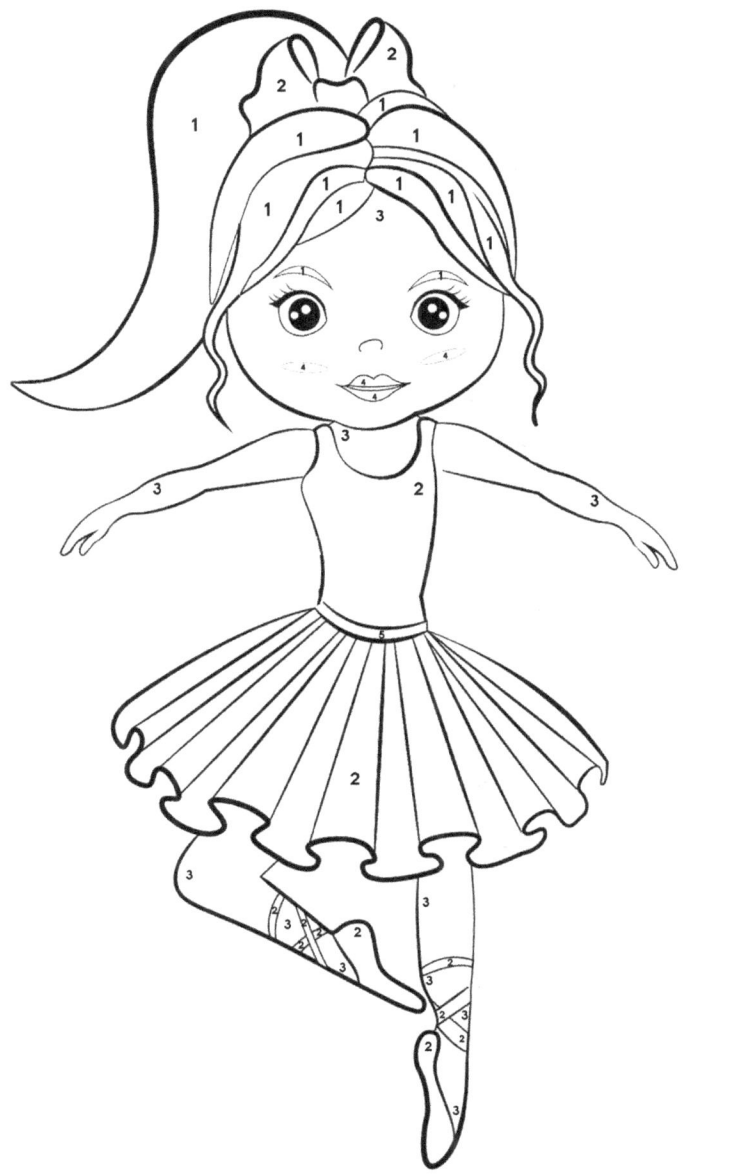

avantgardetheatreofdance.com

Can you connect the dots to complete Grace?

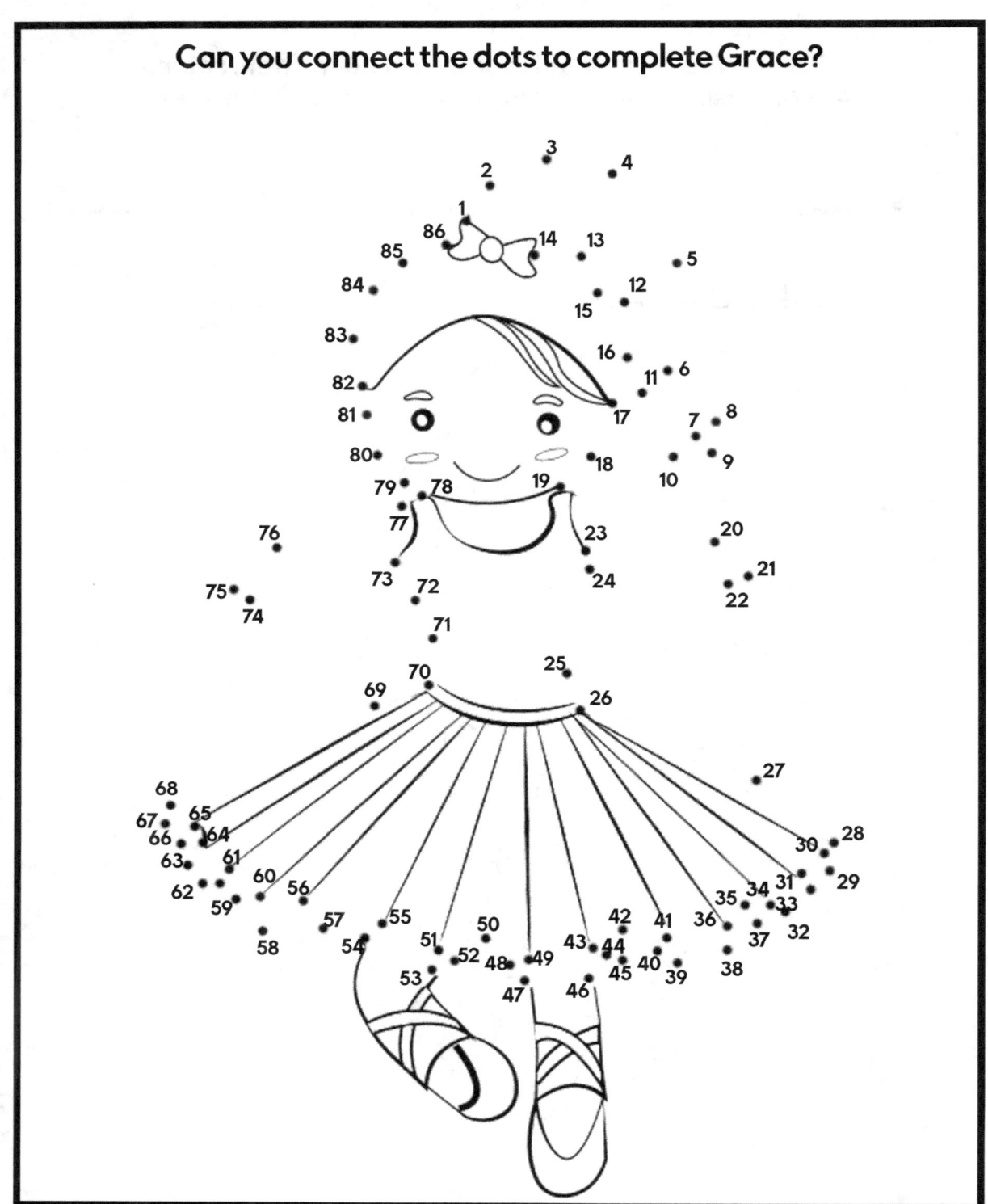

avantgardetheatreofdance.com

Oh no! Aurora lost Grace, can you help Aurora find Grace?

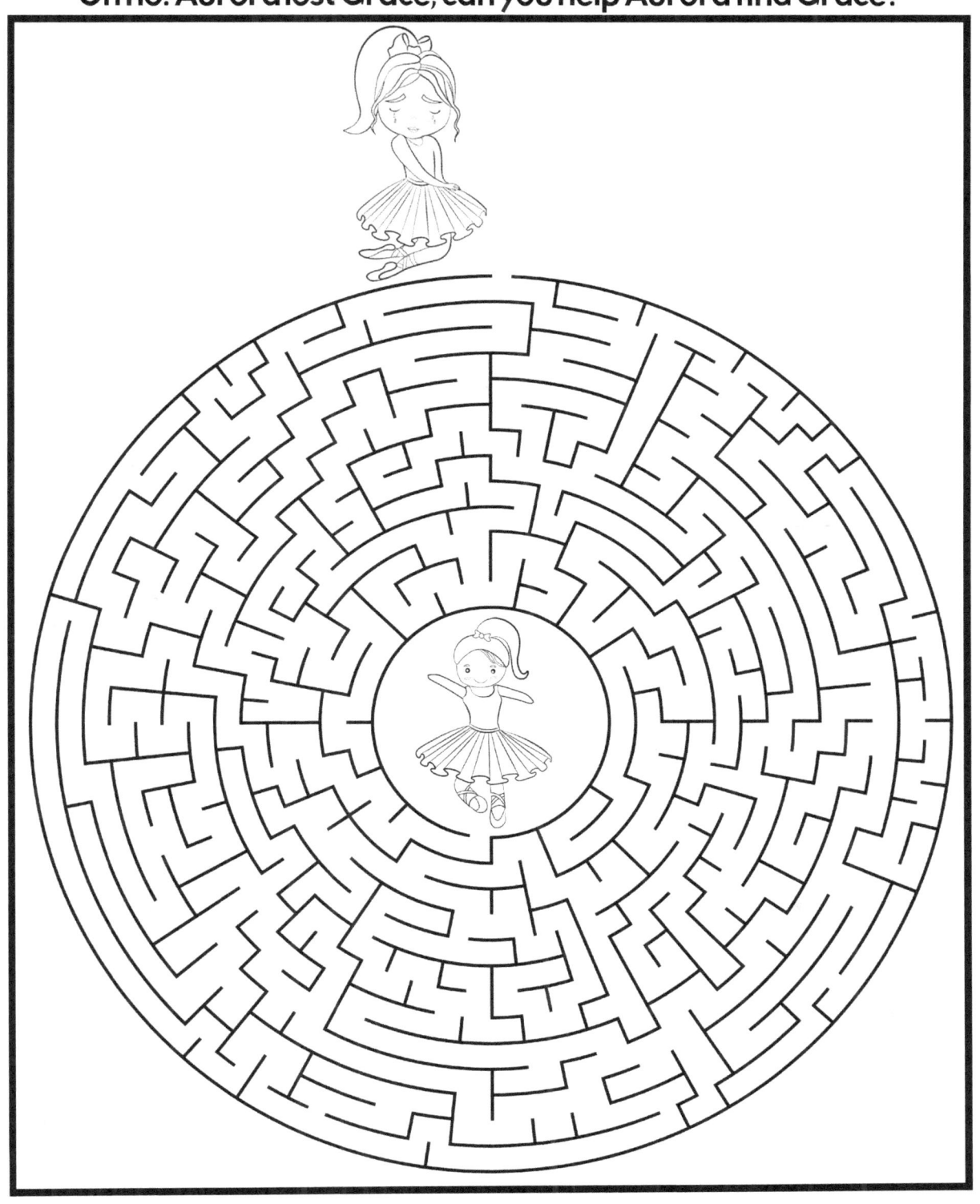

avantgardetheatreofdance.com

Can you remember and spell everyone's names?

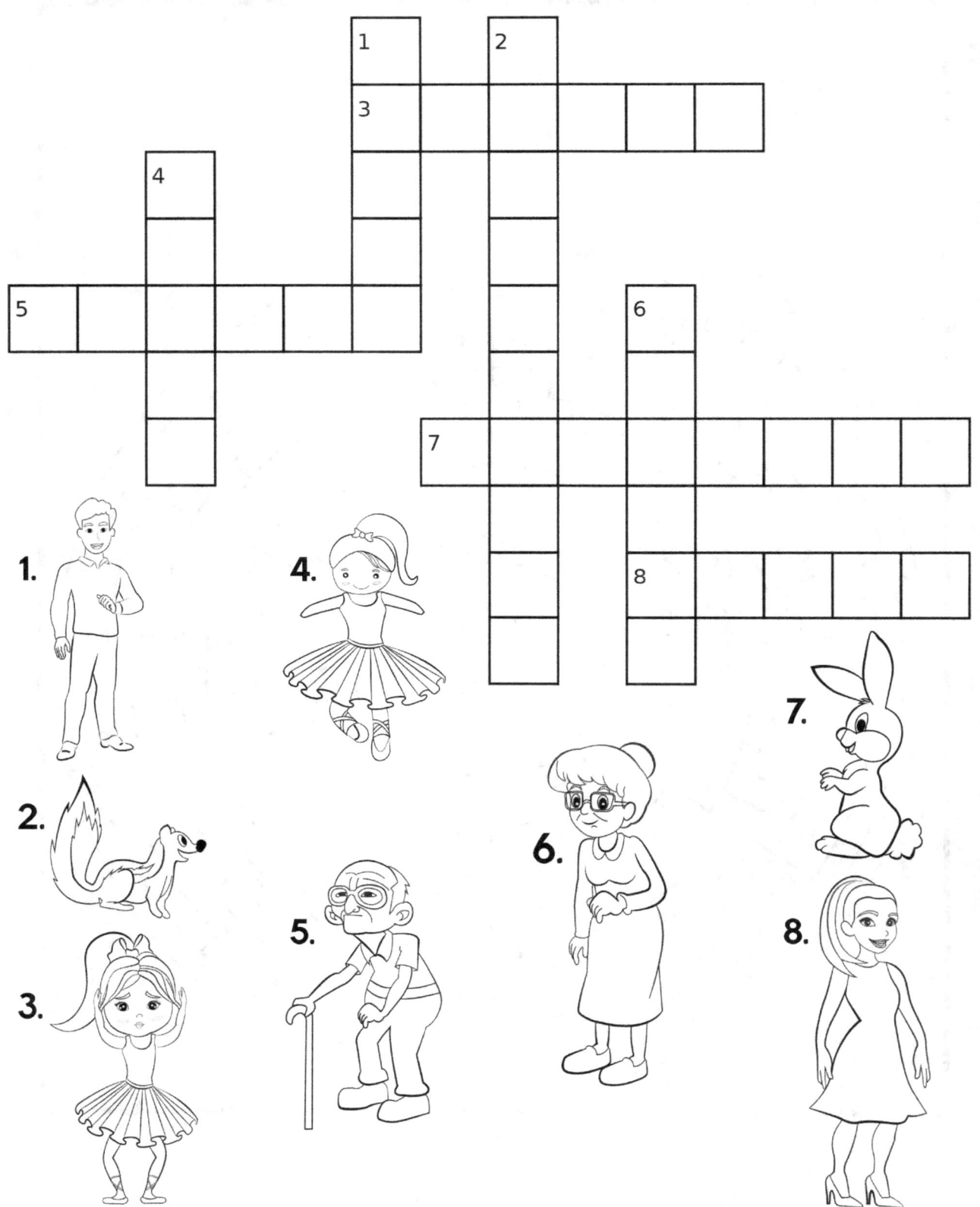

Help Mr. Rabbit and Mr. Squirrel find all of the Ballet Terms!

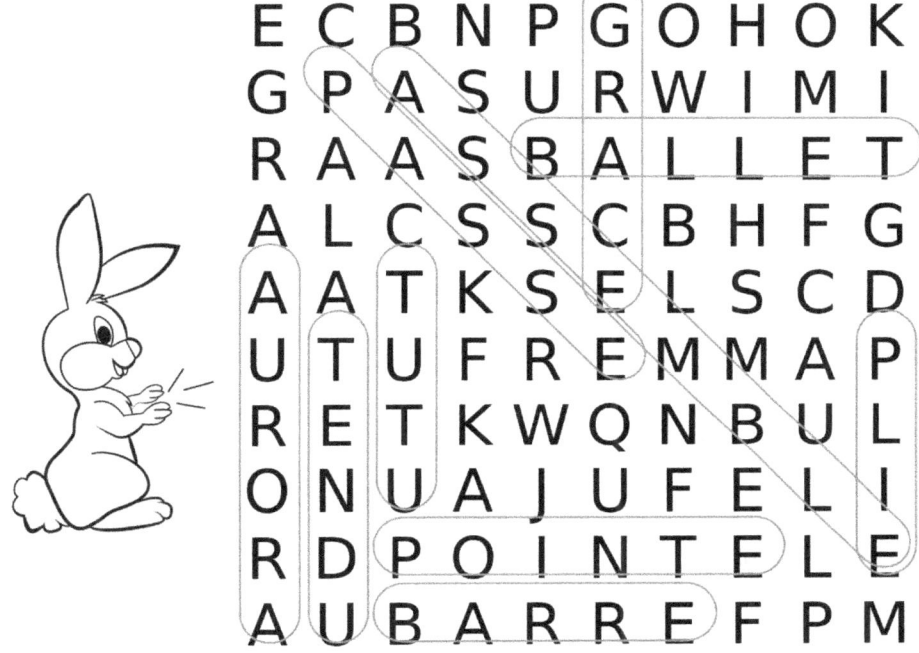

Assemble	Pointe	Ballet	Barre
Passe	Aurora	Tendu	Grace
Plie	Tutu		

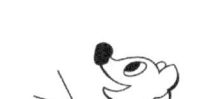

avantgardetheatreofdance.com

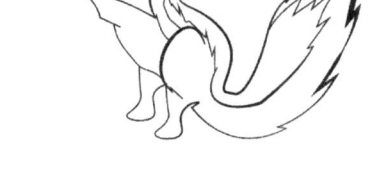

Answer Key

Oh no! Aurora lost Grace, can you help Aurora find Grace?

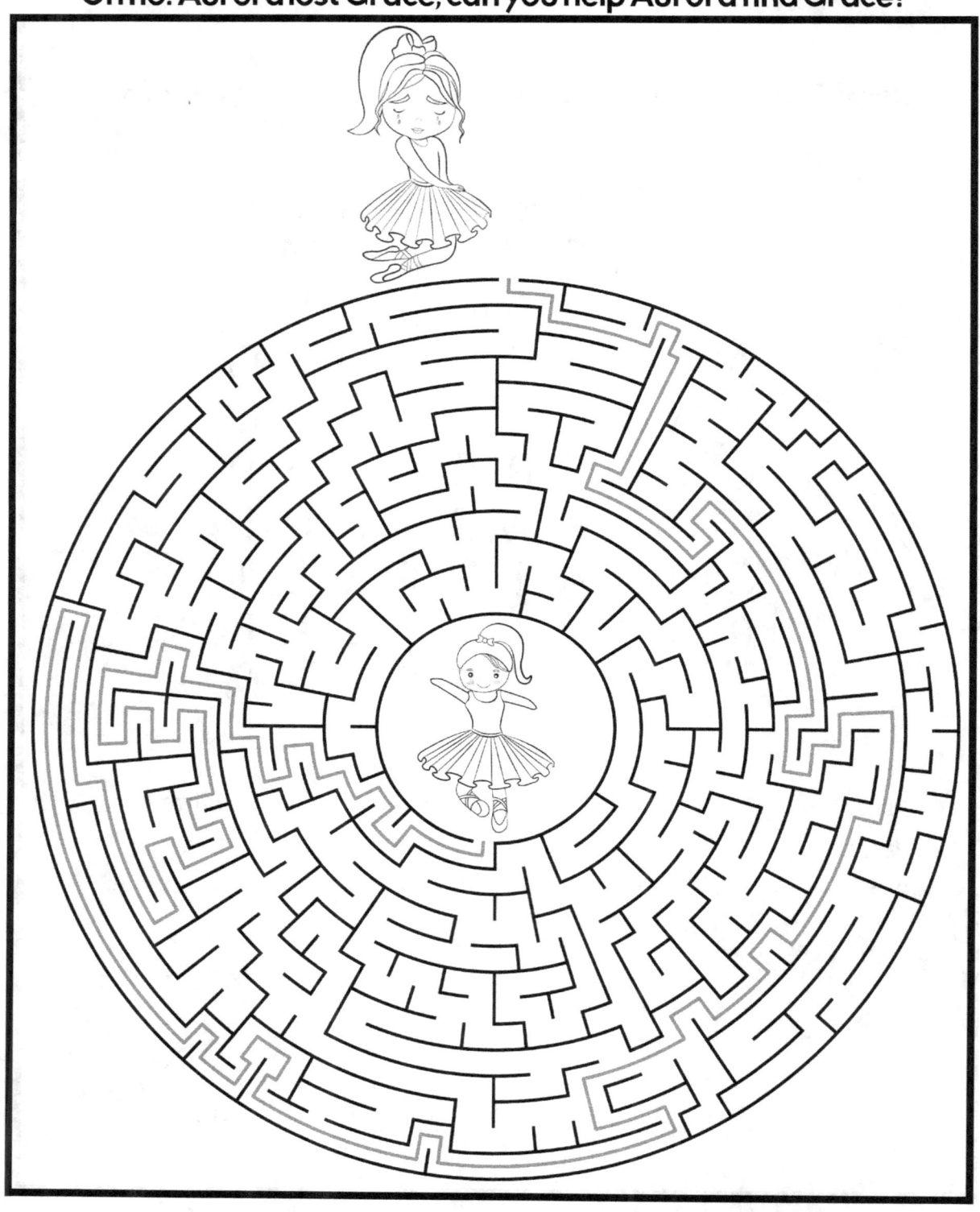

avantgardetheatreofdance.com

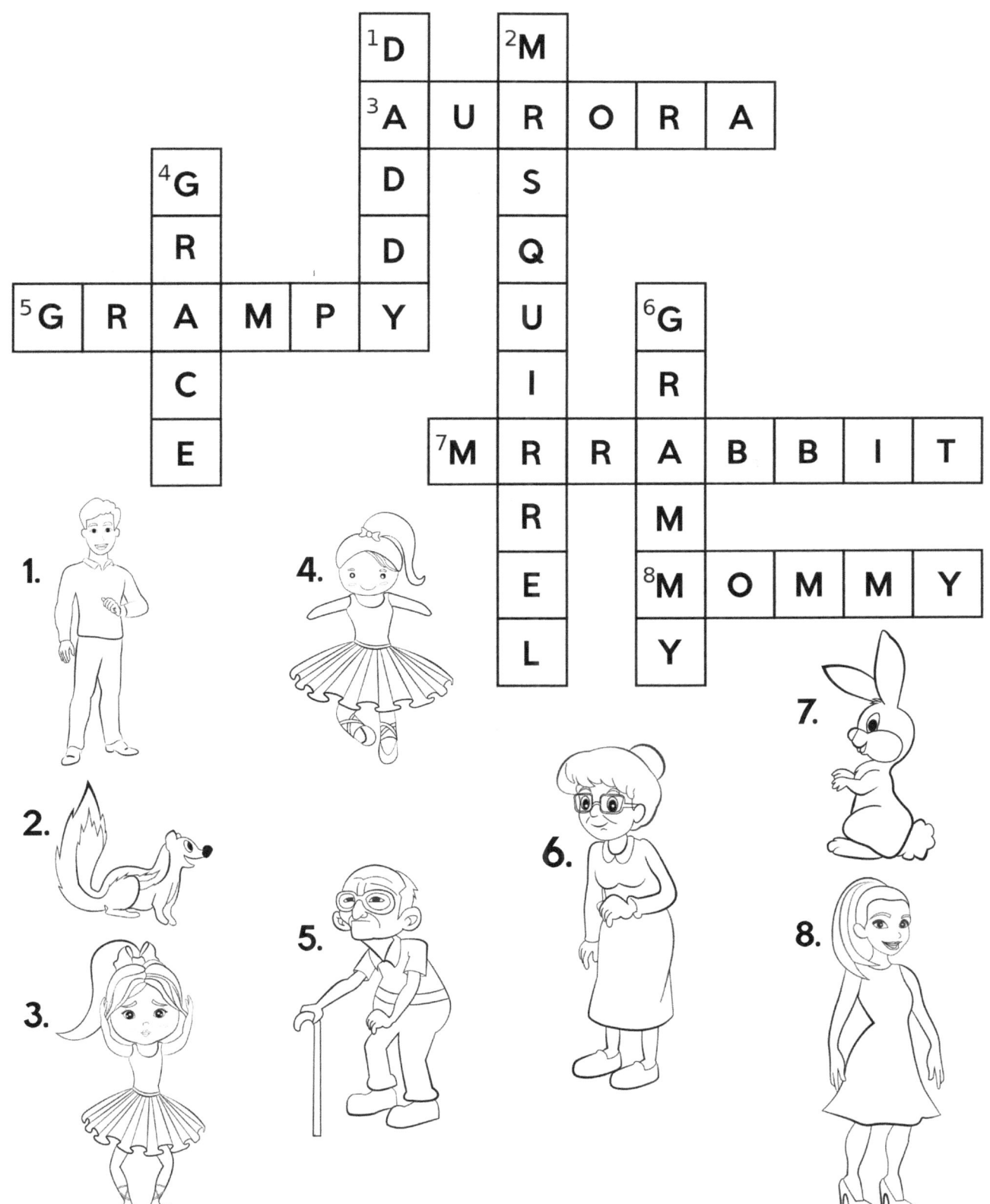

Thank you for supporting Avant Garde Theatre of Dance

Avant Garde Theatre of Dance appreciates and welcomes Sponsorship from supporters who are as passionate about the art of dance in their community as we are.

All donations are used to help support Student Tuition, Competitions, Annual Shows, and more.

Choose from a variety of Sponsorship Packages on our website if you would like to become a Sponsor and help a child fulfil their dreams as a professional dancer!

Visit avantgardetheatreofdance.com/sponsor for more information

© Copyright 2020 Avant Garde Theatre of Dance. All Rights Reserved.

www.ingramcontent.com/pod-product-compliance
Lightning Source LLC
Chambersburg PA
CBHW081710220526
45466CB00009B/2940